A GOLFER'S DAY
WITH THE MASTER

DOUBLEDAY
New York   London   Toronto   Sydney   Auckland

A GOLFER'S DAY
WITH THE MASTER

SPIRITUAL WISDOM FROM
THE FAIRWAY

Marie and Shep!
May the
Divine Master
be your guide,
Love,
Dorothy
Ederer :)

DOROTHY K. EDERER

PUBLISHED BY DOUBLEDAY
a division of Random House, Inc.
1540 Broadway, New York, New York 10036

DOUBLEDAY and the portrayal of an anchor with a
dolphin are trademarks of Doubleday, a division of
Random House, Inc.

BOOK DESIGN AND ILLUSTRATIONS
BY LISA SLOANE

Library of Congress Cataloging-in-Publication

Ederer, Dorothy K.
A golfer's day with the Master: spiritual wisdom
from the fairway/Dorothy K. Ederer—1st ed.
p. cm.
1. Golfers—Religious life.   2. Golf—Religious
aspects—Christianity.   I. Title.
BV4596.G64 E34 2000
242'.68—dc21   99-058553

ISBN 0-385-49995-7

May 2000

FIRST EDITION
1   3   5   7   9   10   8   6   4   2

I dedicate this book to the Divine Master,
the only true professional on life's courses,
who has been my unseen companion
in every game.

I also dedicate it to
Gerri and Joe Navarre
and
Bernie and David Ederer
and all my friends
who enjoy the wonderful game.

My dream is that those who
read this book will also
experience the Master's presence
as they strive to better
their score.

Acknowledgments

There are many friends who have shared stories which have been extremely valuable for the completion of this book.

I want to thank Susan Webber, president of Women on the Green, Nancy Hovis, communication and customer service director of Women on the Green, and Geets Vincent, a freelance writer from California, for their expert advice on sources of information.

I am also grateful to John Block, assistant sportswriter for the *Kalamazoo Gazette*, and Bob McCarthy, vice president of sales at the Upjohn Company.

I appreciate my good friend, Joseph F. Girzone, whose support and affirmation continue to challenge me.

I will always be grateful to my dear friend, Peter Ginsberg, whose faith in me continues to surprise me.

Thanks to my editors at Doubleday, Trace Murphy, who works so patiently with me, and is a dear friend and gentle critic; and Andrew Corbin, for his enthusiasm and creative ideas.

Contents

PRAYERS AND REFLECTIONS

A Golfer's Day
with the Master

Foreword

Games often mimic life, or an aspect of life.
Golf is one game that can be easily sublimated,
which can in itself be fun.

In this delightful little book of reflections,
Dorothy K. Ederer cleverly utilizes the jargon and
artful strategies of golf to playfully refocus attention
on important things in life.

The way golfers play the game, and the way they
react to people and events in the game often reflects
the way they react to people and events in their
everyday life. Our relationship with God and family
and friends are just a few.

I know readers will enjoy immensely these poignant
and whimsical reflections. They will also find them-
selves enjoying, perhaps for the first time, praying.

— JOSEPH F. GIRZONE

Introduction

As we reflect on our game, may we be conscious of the Divine Master, who is always there to guide us and help us find the missing links in life.

The prayers and stories for each hole come from the heart of a person whose spirit is energized by the game.

Hopefully, the other prayers and reflections will lift our minds to God and enhance our concentration.

My "beatitudes" in the following pages are happy ways of looking at the whimsical coincidences that have occurred to those whose spirit was open to see the Master's humor.

The "psalms" and "ten commandments" for the golfer remind us of our need to listen to the voice within as well as that of the Master. Of all the sports, golf is the one game that has no scapegoats. As we play, we learn more about ourselves, how we react to our shots and our final score, and what may be going on in our lives. It also tells us about how we approach life.

Golf is also a humbling sport as it frustrates while it challenges. It also provides delightful opportunities to spend three or four hours not only enjoying the beauty of God's creation, but having fun walking and talking with friends.

May this book help you focus on good qualities and accept your handicaps with humor.

Reflections as You Walk the Course

Before Your Game

Divine Master, thank You for offering to be
　　　　our caddie in life and allowing
　　　　our friendship
　　　　to be based on winter rules.

As we walk the course today,
　　　　we look forward to Your company,
　　　　especially as we search
　　　　in the woods
　　　　and wander off course.
Each hole is a time to reflect
　　　　on Your presence.

No matter how badly we play, help us get past
　　　　the red tees.
We will try to face ourselves honestly
　　　　and not be discouraged
　　　　by our handicaps
　　　　or the hazards that haunt us.

As we go from one fairway to another,
        may Your presence become more intimate
        so when we reach the end of the game,
whether we win or lose,
        we will feel ourselves closer to You
        than when the game began.

Psalm 139 for the Golfer

Divine Master, You have watched me and
    You know me.
You know when I duff and when I divot.
You understand my plays from afar.
My swings and my putts You scrutinize,
    with all my strokes You are familiar.
As soon as the ball takes flight,
    behold, Wise Master,
    You know its destination.

Behind me and before me, You help me swing,
    and rest Your hand upon mine.
Such comfort is too wonderful for me, too lofty
    for me to comprehend.

Who knows the course of the ball in flight?
If it goes into the waters, You are there.
If it sinks into the sand trap, You are there.
If I wander into barren wasteland,
        even there Your hand shall guide me,
        to help me score my best.

Probe me, O God, and know my heart,
        try me and know my thoughts.
See if my way is crooked,
        and lead me, if not to a hole in one,
        at least to a praiseworthy finish.

Hole 1

I WILL LEAD THE BLIND ON THEIR JOURNEY; BY
PATHS UNKNOWN I WILL GUIDE THEM. I WILL
TURN THE DARKNESS INTO LIGHT BEFORE THEM.

—ISAIAH 42:16

*Divine Master, every now and then we meet
extraordinary people. Greg Matthew, a
golf pro and owner of the Pine View
golf course in Kalamazoo, allowed us to
take blind students cross-country skiing
on his course.*

Greg became a pro in 1956. He was always a
par golfer, but when he lost his sight in 1970
from diabetes, he continued to golf and broke
an eighty-six or better every time. In 1980 the
doctors amputated his right leg. Still he continued to play, happy to break one hundred. In
1996 he had a heart attack while golfing but
that, too, didn't stop him.

On December 11, 1998, he was hospitalized for numerous complications. By his bedside were his wife, Jan, his children, Lisa and Tim, and Tim's wife, Lynn. Greg was lying peacefully when all of a sudden, he took off his oxygen mask, looked up at his family, and smiled. He saw them for the first time in twenty-eight years. He then asked his wife to kiss him and, after a deep sigh, breathed his last and went home to the Divine Master.

Afterward, his wife told me, "For the first time in twenty-eight years, he could see us. His eyes were no longer covered by a gray film, but were as clear as a blue sky. I know it was a miracle."

God, You continue to bless us with miracles,
    most of which pass unnoticed.
Shield us from discouragement when tragedy
    knocks at the door.
Give us the courage as you did Greg,
    to go on
    when all seems hopeless.

Hole 2

PRAY FOR US; WE ARE CONFIDENT THAT WE HAVE
A GOOD CONSCIENCE, WISHING, AS WE DO, TO
ACT RIGHTLY IN EVERY RESPECT.

—HEBREWS 13:18

*O God, it's not easy to be honest when we think
we may lose what we aspired for most in
life. Bobby Jones showed great integrity
in a situation like this.*

In the 1925 U.S. Open, his ball moved when
he addressed it. No one else had seen it move,
but Bobby did and he had to be honest. He
called the penalty on himself, which cost him
the championship.

When asked, "Why did you do that?" he
responded, "There's only one way to play the
game. You might as well praise a man for not

robbing a bank as to praise him for playing by the rules."

Divine Master, it cost him the game, but he was
        admired by millions
        for his good sportsmanship,
        even today.
Teach me always to be honest with myself
        and others.
Help me to let go of what is not of my doing,
        and accept what is my fault.
Thank You, God, for accepting me
        and loving me
        when I make mistakes.
Help me to forgive myself.

A wise person said, "If you're honest,
        you'll have the inner peace
        which so many seek."
God, I want that inner peace which comes from
        being honest.

Hole 3

**WHAT THE WICKED ONE FEARS WILL BEFALL HIM,
BUT THE DESIRE OF THE JUST WILL BE GRANTED.**

—PROVERBS 10:24

*Divine Master, Tony Morrone and
      Larry Bertoli, two good friends
      and golfers, love to tell stories.
      Here's one you'll enjoy.*

This incident took place in 1915. It made
us aware that You most probably had a hand
in it.

The president of the Lakeside Country Club,
in Tacoma, Dan McDonald, was playing his
first hole there. He had a good drive, but the
mashie pitch went wild and struck the side of
a cow that had wandered onto the course.
Smarting from the blow, the cow kicked and
struck the ball just as it hit the ground, send-

ing it onto the green. One putt won the hole.
Justice DeWitt M. Evans was there to witness
the incident.

God, we so often see Your humor as we live
        each day.
        You enjoy surprising us with
        bizarre situations like this.
They bring joy to our weary spirits.

What happened to Dan was more than
        he anticipated.

Thank You for the delightful little surprises
        You send our way.
I pray that I may always be grateful,
        because it is in those unexpected blessings
        that Your presence becomes real.

Hole 4

LET EVERYONE BE QUICK TO HEAR, SLOW TO
SPEAK, AND SLOW TO ANGER.

—JAMES 1:19B

*God, You must cringe every time you hear Your
name or other words used in vain on the
course. Teach us to think before we
speak, especially when we find ourselves
in situations like the following:*

It was the annual All Saints Regional High
School Golf Outing at Old Brookville
Country Club in Long Island. Tom Connolly
had a chance to play with home office people
from one of the insurance companies he rep-
resents. One of the representatives, Bill, a
gentle man, was playing six over par at the
time. They were on the sixteenth hole. Bill
was setting up to take his tee shot; as he
raised his club to swing, a beautiful water

spaniel appeared out of nowhere, ran up to the ball, grabbed it, and took off. Bill was shocked. As quickly as the dog came, he left, returning the ball back near the tee, then stood off to the side. Bill, upset with the distraction, set up again. The dog repeated the action three more times, but the third time Bill took a different ball and threw it in the direction of another tee nearby. The dog took the cue and dashed off to the other tee, where a man was getting ready to tee off. The dog repeated his act for the other man. Bill quickly made his hit and finished his game. His golfing partners still laugh as they share the incident.

If you are humble and do not take your game too seriously, then you would enjoy playing with someone like this: Joe, with his foursome, was golfing at the Marriott in Bermuda. His ball landed in the fountain at the eighteenth hole. Unperturbed, he was determined to retrieve it. He took off his shoes and socks and stepped in. "Look at all the balls in here. Wow, this is heaven," he yelled to his partner. Then he proceeded to collect them in his shirt.

Their two women companions were so embarrassed, they finished their putts and returned to the clubhouse. Minutes later Joe and his partner arrived. They were like two little kids, showing everyone all the golf balls they had found. People at the clubhouse will never forget Joe.

Divine Master, grant us the gifts of humility
and patience needed
when golfing with others.
Help us avoid becoming angry
or annoyed at the bizarre
things that happen on the course.
Teach us how to be humble
when golfing with someone
who doesn't take the game too seriously.

Hole 5

WHILE FROM BEHIND, A VOICE SHALL SOUND IN
YOUR EARS; "THIS IS THE WAY; WALK IN IT,"
WHEN YOU WOULD TURN TO THE RIGHT OR TO
THE LEFT.

—ISAIAH 30:21

*Divine Master, the Sise brothers who manage
Briar Creek golf course in Upstate New
York, make everyone feel welcome. They
have many interesting stories to tell.
Here are a few.*

Freddie Tait, a Scottish amateur, discovered
after a shot that his ball had landed inside a
small, condensed-milk can. Instead of taking
an unplayable lie, he just swung at the can.
Much to his surprise, it landed on the green.
The ball rolled out, stopping right next to the
hole.

Byron Nelson, from Texas, was assistant pro at Ridgewood, a fine country club in New Jersey. A member of the club asked him if he could hit a flagpole that was off in the distance. So Byron took a one iron and aimed. The ball flew through the air and, to everyone's surprise, hit the pole. Years later he won the 1942 Masters against Ben Hogan.

O God, sometimes we accomplish
*   the unexplainable*
*   and shock ourselves.*
In these moments of inconceivable events
*   I become more aware of Your presence*
*   in my life.*
Everything is a gift from You.

Teach me to rejoice in the present moment,
*   and not*
*   take anything for granted.*

Hole 6

DON'T BE AFRAID, BECAUSE I HAVE SAVED YOU.
I HAVE CALLED YOU BY NAME, AND YOU ARE MINE.

—ISAIAH 43:1

Divine Master, each of us was created for a special purpose, and no matter what handicaps we may have, You will achieve your plan through us, if we are willing to let go and trust. These two men's disability did not stop them from allowing Your plan to be accomplished.

In 1954 Ed Furgol, with his crippled arm, won the U.S. Open.

In 1998 Casey Martin, who has a rare disease that would eventually cause him to lose his leg, fought the golf establishment and won the right to play golf in the PGA tournaments

and ride in a golf cart. Today he competes
against the world's best golfers on the PGA
Tour, even though he has a crippled leg.

God, it is so difficult to believe we can achieve
things we really want when we have a
disability.
These two men have inspired many
to pursue a dream,
even when all the odds
were against them.
If we can trust
and put our faith in You,
anything can happen.

Hole 7

As for clothes, why be concerned?

—MATTHEW 6:28

Divine Master, we know you'll be there to guide us no matter how we appear to others.

I laughed when Tracy Egan, a golfer and anchor woman at Channel 10 in Albany, New York shared this story. Margaret Abbott, an American, was visiting Paris as the 1900 Olympic Games were about to begin. She was not an official U.S. athlete, but she was allowed to enter the women's golf competition. Not having proper attire, she golfed in high-heel shoes and a short skirt. She was the first woman to win an Olympic gold medal.

O God, we admire Margaret for accepting a
        challenge and not
        being afraid of possible ridicule.
Help us not to be concerned about
        what others think
        or how we look,
        but be secure in
        who we are.

Every day we face circumstances
        that are challenging,
        we can either ignore or embrace them.
But when we respond to the unthinkable,
        our life can become
        a wonderful adventure!

Hole 8

DEDICATE YOUR LIVES TO THANKFULNESS.

—COLOSSIANS 3:15B

Divine Master, sometimes You bless us with those unexpected blessings, and a simple "thank you" seems empty. These two men were thrilled at what happened to them.

In Santa Ana, California, during a 1977 round at the River View golf course, Dean Colbert, with a little nudge from his brother, made a hole in one at the ninth hole.

Dean hit the ball first and it landed inches from the cup. His brother, Ken, followed with a drive that looked just like his brother's. Ken's ball nudged Dean's into the cup. Match-play rules at the time stipulated a golfer had a choice—replace the ball in its original lie or accept its new position. Well, we all know that Dean didn't have to think twice. He accepted the ace graciously and thanked the Master.

During the Depression in 1930, in order to keep the course open, the city of Portland offered lifetime memberships at any of the municipal courses for one hundred dollars. They sold two hundred life passes. Little did they know that Lou Rose, who bought a life pass, would still be using it today.

"There are a couple of others still alive, but he is the only one still playing at the Eastmoreland golf course," said Clark Pumpston, the golf pro.

Divine Master, there are so many little things
that happen to us each day
that we are grateful for.
Inspire us to take time to give thanks for the
many blessings
that come our way.

Hole 9

THAT RESOURCEFULNESS MAY BE IMPARTED TO
THE SIMPLE, TO A YOUNG PERSON'S KNOWLEDGE
AND DISCRETION.

—PROVERBS 1:4

*Divine Master, when we meet a generous person
we can't help but wish we were more
giving. Often the expression of goodwill
means more to the person than the help
we actually give. But in this situation,
Lee Trevino's help was a blessing to those
desperately in need.*

In 1971 Lee Trevino won the British Open at
Royal Birkdale. The people running the
tournament told him that it was a tradition
for the champion to give a portion of his
check to the local Catholic orphanage.
He agreed to give fifteen hundred dollars,
but on one condition. The nuns from the

orphanage had to come and have a glass of champagne with him at the nearby Kingway Casino. Naturally the sisters agreed, even though they had never been in the casino or had ever had a drink. Lee was so touched by it all that he auctioned off the clubs he used to win the Open and donated the proceeds, another fifteen hundred dollars, to the kids at the orphanage.

O God, what a glorious day for the sisters!
Lee's generosity
won their hearts.
The children at the orphanage
realized that not only would their
physical needs be taken care of,
but they knew they were loved.
That made
a difference.

Lee Trevino is admired not only by those sisters,
   but by many others today
   who hear this story,
   whether they are golfers
   or not.

O God, help me to give when there is a need,
   without expecting
   anything in return.

Hole 10

WHEN YOU PASS THROUGH THE WATERS, I WILL
BE WITH YOU. WHEN YOU CROSS RIVERS YOU
WILL NOT DROWN.

—ISAIAH 43:1–2

*God, whenever there is water along the course,
my ball is sure to find it.*

In 1988 I was golfing with Jackie Sanders and
John Grathwohl when my ball plunged into a
pond off the first green at the Elks in
Kalamazoo.

Jackie, a young college student yelled, "I'll get
it!" She bent over to retrieve the ball, her feet
slipped and she plunged head first into the
muddy waters.

John laughed so hard he fell to the ground.
"I've never seen anything like this!" he said.

Giggling, I said to Jackie, "Are you all right?"

Seconds later, Jackie popped out of the water, her body draped in weeds and muck, and held the ball in the air, laughing. "I got it! I got it!"

That year she received a ball retriever for graduation.

God, Your humor shows in many little ways.
> *As Jackie,*
> *covered with mud and weeds,*
> *could laugh at herself*
> *as she held the ball high,*
> *may we always*
> *see humor*
> *in stressful times.*

Life is meant to be embraced, enjoyed, and
> *celebrated!*

Hole 11

SO, BE TRULY GLAD! THERE IS A WONDERFUL JOY
AHEAD, EVEN THOUGH THE GOING IS ROUGH . . .

—1 PETER 1:6

Divine Master, my expectations are high,
*   and I become discouraged*
*   when I don't do as well*
*   as I think I should.*
Sometimes I get so caught up with achievement
*   that I forget*
*   not only the rules but the role that You*
*   play in my success.*

In the 1959 Chicago Open, Billy Casper hit his
tee shot into the middle of a thick mulberry bush
at the eleventh hole. He was not aware that he
could have taken a free drop. It took him ten
strokes to free the ball. He lost the Open by
three strokes.

Wise Master, how many times have I been
      unaware of rules
      or forgot to read instructions because
      of the excitement of the moment?

It is difficult to give up, especially when
      You believe
      You can do it.
We can all identify with Billy in his
      determination to accomplish
      what he set out to do.

Knowing the rules of the game can help us
      avoid these
      frustrating moments.

Help me to continue to struggle
      when things get rough
      and to realize You are there to help me in
      times of need.

I need Your grace to help me reflect on Your presence
      in tough situations.

Hole 12

THERE IS NO LIMIT TO LOVE'S FORBEARANCE, TO ITS TRUST, ITS HOPE, ITS POWER TO ENDURE.

—I CORINTHIANS 13:7

Divine Master, love is relentless. It calls us to accept challenges when we are not always sure of the outcome, as in this situation with Arnold Palmer.

Arnie was just out of the Coast Guard, but already had a great reputation as an amateur golfer. He wanted to get married, but he didn't have enough money to buy Winnie an engagement ring.

Some of his friends said they'd pay him one hundred dollars for every stroke he made under par seventy-two at the Pine Valley course in Clementon, New Jersey. But, for every stroke over eighty, he would have to pay them one hundred dollars. Arnie scored a sixty-eight. Well, you know the rest. He was so excited he went out and bought her the ring, and they lived happily ever after.

Divine Master, love like that is a God-given
      love to be celebrated.
To love another is to make God's love visible to
      the world.

We come alive when we know we are loved and
      accepted
      for who we are.
We then find ourselves looking at others with
      new eyes, and with
      kinder and more forgiving hearts.

O God, teach me to love as You do. As I learn
      to give more of
      myself, I learn how to love more
      unselfishly.

I pray that all my relationships will
      come alive
      through Your spirit.

Hole 13

A CHEERFUL GLANCE BRINGS JOY TO THE HEART;
GOOD NEWS INVIGORATES THE BONES.

—PROVERBS 15:30

*God, so many people are gifted in golf,
including many young people like the
following.*

Tiger Woods has been blessed with an incredible gift for golf. He swung his first golf club when he was six months old. At two he was matching putts with Bob Hope on *The Mike Douglas Show.* At three, he played his first round of golf and shot a forty-eight for nine holes. Some people get excited when they get a score like that for nine holes who've been playing for years. He continues to soar on the courses.

A twenty-five-year-old South Korean woman, Se Ri Pak, won the United States Women's

Open and the Jamie Farr Kroger Classic. She shot a round of sixty-one, the lowest score ever in the Ladies Professional Golf Association, and finished twenty-three under par. Her role model is Nancy Lopez, who has won a total of forty-eight tournaments in her career. She admires Nancy for being a fantastic golfer and for her smile and happy spirit.

God, we all have gifts and talents,
       but encouragement,
       a person's smile,
       and positive attitude
       can bring
       joy to the human heart.
       Bringing joy and inspiration
       to others is also a great gift.

People are searching for acceptance and love,
        and a smile
        tells a lonely person
        that someone cares.
We all want to make a difference,
        but often
        we do not know how.
Sometimes it takes only
        a word of encouragement
        to one who is gifted and talented.
        To acknowledge
        and support others
        can give them the hope
        needed to continue.
For some that's all it takes.

Hole 14

I ASSURE YOU, IF YOU HAVE FAITH THE SIZE OF A
MUSTARD SEED, YOU WOULD BE ABLE TO SAY TO
THIS MOUNTAIN, "MOVE FROM HERE TO THERE,"
AND IT WOULD MOVE.

—MATTHEW 18:20

*Divine Master, after hearing this story, I found
myself singing "We Walk by Faith."**

Sister Lisa Marie's dad, Chuck Lazio, a golfer
since he was sixteen, went legally blind from
macular degeneration in 1980. His six daugh-
ters (four are nuns, two golfers) weren't sure if
he'd want to golf again.

"I may be blind, but I can't stop living." he
said. "I'm still going to play golf."

*Marty Haugen

He continued to play and got a hole in one five times—one at the Gulf Gate course, and four at the Village Green in Sarasota, Florida. At eighty-seven he suffered a stroke on the golf course. Even after his retirement he continued to inspire others, especially his grandson, a golfer and pilot, not to give up no matter what obstacles come their way.

Divine Master, Chuck walked by faith,
*   not by sight.*
Thank You for Your presence in people like him,
*   who allow Your love and goodness*
*   to radiate.*
Thank You for those who have shown
*   compassion and hope*
*   during weary and bleak moments.*
*   Thank You for assuring us*
*   that You are with us*
*   when we are lonely and lost.*
Thank You for teaching us patience
*   as we continue to search*
*   for our way in life.*

Hole 15

GIVE HER A REWARD OF HER LABORS, AND LET
HER WORKS PRAISE HER AT THE CITY GATES.

—PROVERBS 31:31

*Divine Master, a passage in the Book of
Proverbs describes the ideal woman:
"She makes garments and sells them, and
stocks the merchants with belts. She is
clothed with strength and dignity, and
she laughs at the days to come. She
opens her mouth in wisdom, and on her
tongue is kindly counsel."*

In ages past, that was the ideal woman. Consider
the following as an ideal woman for our time. She
started golfing at twenty-one, and soon became
an assistant pro. She was the LPGA tournament
director and gained a lifetime membership in the
LPGA teaching division. She was an FAA certified
flight and ground school instructor, and owned

ten different planes. She received an impressive award from Foothill College, where she taught aviation for eighteen years. She was elected to the International Women's Sports Hall of Fame. At seventy-eight she took part in her own tournament for single professional women, which she sponsored for twenty-four years. She has published three books—two on golf and one on cooking. She is a skilled artist who has done exquisite drawings of LPGA and Hollywood notables, and has played the cello since age twelve. She is a golfer, historian, teacher, writer, artist, musician. Betty Hicks has earned a place in our hearts and in the history of golf. She surely is a model woman for our times.

Divine Master, we are grateful to You
for the people
who love us and challenge us to
new and exciting adventures.
Enlighten us to know our gifts and talents
and teach us how
to overcome the fear of
sharing them.

Hole 16

LET US RUN THE RACE THAT IS BEFORE US AND
NEVER GIVE UP.

—HEBREWS 12:1

*Divine Master, the following people were
determined never to abandon their
dreams. With Your constant help they
succeeded wonderfully.*

Babe Zaharias, an American athlete, excelled
in many sports. She won a place on the All-
American women's basketball team and three
national records in track and field events. She
set records for the javelin throw and the
eighty-meter hurdle. She won two gold
medals and a silver in the Olympics. She then
decided to take up golf, and from 1936 to
1954 won the British and U.S. Women's
Amateur, four world championships, and three
U.S. Women's Opens before she died from

cancer. She was one of the founding members of the LPGA. She has been considered by many one of the most outstanding women athletes of the twentieth century.

Nancy Lopez is easily the greatest woman golfer of our time. At her peak, she could drive the ball an average of 265 yards. She has won forty-eight tournaments, including every major except the Open. She has recently accepted the USGA's Bob Jones Award, the most prestigious award in golf. She is one of only nine to receive it. Nancy is the only member of the Hall of Fame to get there while raising a family. She is the first woman to create and launch clubs specifically designed under her name.

Jack Nicklaus, an outstanding golfer and a legend of our time, has been a great inspiration to the younger generation. Often it is difficult for people who have been pros in any particular field to watch the younger generation rise to fame. What is so nice about Jack is

that he rejoices when younger golfers succeed, as long as they are good role models for
our young people. It has always been important in his golf and in his life.

Don Pooley, who aced the 192-yard seven-
teenth hole at the Hertz Bay Classic in
Orlando, would never give up. The hole in
one gave him a half-million-dollar bonus,
which has been known as the largest single-
hole prize in golf history.

Divine Master, these people wouldn't give up
*   on their dream.*
Their determination and dedication
*   brought them where they are today.*

May we place our trust in You and avoid
*   any anxiety or worry*
*   as we walk joyfully with You*
*   down the fairway of life.*
Grant us the insight to recognize
*   the blessings that come our way.*

Hole 17

**ENTRUST YOUR WORKS TO THE LORD, AND YOUR
PLANS WILL SUCCEED.**

—PROVERBS 16:3

*Divine Master, You inspired the following
people to share their love for those
suffering from a disability. It is
incredible how quickly we recover
when we are loved and affirmed.*

Bev Regan and Laura Giandomenico, thera-
peutic recreation specialists, discovered how
lessons about balance and range of motion are
surprisingly similar to the lessons golf
professionals teach. They contacted Mike
Olizarevitch, a golf pro at the city-owned
Fanshawe Golf and Country Club, in London,
Ontario, which has two regulation eighteen-
courses and a nine-hole course called Parkside

Nine for the handicapped. It is the only golf course he knows of in North America that is designed specifically for the physically challenged. The holes are fifty to one hundred and fifty yards long and entirely wheelchair accessible.

Mike enlisted two fellow pros, Fred Kern and Andy Shaw, also unpaid volunteers, to help. Twenty clinics have proven successful by combining rehabilitation efforts with golf techniques. Some of the participants could make shots and putts even if they were amputees, spinal-cord injured, or otherwise wheelchair bound.

Mike said, "We are making a difference. I worked with a stroke patient, and after six weeks of therapy, he was playing the course. It's so rewarding, instilling confidence and seeing them progress so fast. One of my greatest joys is seeing the smiles on their faces. I tell them, 'If you can dream it, you can do it.' We hold special events here and are

opening the course this year for children,
three to nine, so they can start playing."

Divine Master, it is difficult to know what You
        have in mind for
        each of us.
When we use our gifts to encourage others
        to become better,
        it's amazing the effect it has on us.

Standing by a dreamer's side
        and working with him
        as he takes his first steps
        is one of the most rewarding experiences.

Encourage us to respond to the spirit within
        so we can bring life to those
        who may be losing hope.

Hole 18

Divine Master, it is a miracle how Ben Hogan and his wife survived a nearly fatal auto accident.

While Ben was bending over to save his wife's life, his left leg was crushed, his ankle fractured, and his pelvis and left collarbone were broken. Because of head injuries, he was visually impaired. Complications set in, blood clots in his left leg migrated to his lungs, and the doctors didn't think he would live. Emergency surgery saved his life, but he would always have pain in his legs.

After spending two months in the hospital, it was seven months before he could hit a golf ball again. Sixteen months later he entered the U.S. Open. He was in so much pain, he could hardly stand up after each swing. He almost quit because he didn't think he could walk the final eighteen holes, but he continued to wrap his legs, and stayed to finish. Ben was able to stand the test and come back and win six times in the most prestigious golf tournaments in the world: three U.S. Opens, two Masters, and a British Open.

Divine Healer, I admire Ben's determination
and courage to continue to go on when
all seemed hopeless.
His determination and dedication are an
inspiration.

Changes in our life are very difficult
to accept at times.
Shield me from any harm
and help me to be patient with myself
as I find my way in this world.

Hole 19

THERE IS CAUSE FOR REJOICING HERE.

—I PETER 1:6

Divine Master, finishing our game, we
approach the nineteenth hole with
anticipation. This reminds me of the
final nineteenth hole of life as we arrive
at Your banquet, where the joy and
celebration will be out of this world.

As we approached the nineteenth hole one
day, we had great reason to celebrate. It was a
beautiful sunny day in June at the Ridgeview
golf course in Kalamazoo, Michigan. Kathy
and Lowell Rinker, Jackie and Gary Shuk, and
I had just finished a fun afternoon of golf.

At the beginning, Lowell, as usual, had has-
sled the women about the unfairness of the

distance between the women's and men's tee. As we approached the tenth tee, Lowell was still going on. "You girls got it made, twenty yards before you even shoot."

"We're just trying to follow the rules, but if that's the way you feel, I'll play from the men's tee." I said.

He laughed. "This should be interesting," he said.

I took my five wood (which Lowell had made for me) and a Slazenger ball (from a friend, Jim Merna). Gary threw me a red tee, saying, "Here, you'll need all the help you can get."

Giggling, I tried to compose myself. I swung and the ball sailed off into the air. I didn't even bother looking, but walked over to put my club into the bag.

Gary yelled, "It went in! It went in! She got a hole in one."

Lowell laughed. "No way, you've got to be joking."

"Honest, I saw it go in!" said Gary.

Thinking they were making fun, I ignored them and got in my cart and waited for Jackie and Kathy to tee off.

As we all proceeded up the fairway, Lowell still joked about the disappearing ball, until we reached the green. I stood there, stunned. "It did go in, it did go in!" I shouted.

"I told you it did," Gary said in desperation.

"Well, Dort, I have to take the ball," Jackie said.

"No way, that ball brought me luck."

"But that's the rule. The ball has to be retired," she insisted.

Reluctantly, I gave her the ball.

Then Lowell started in again. "Now listen, sis, you really didn't have much to do with this, you know."

"What do you mean by that?" I said.

"Well, I made you the club, Jim gave you the Slazenger ball, Gary gave you the tee. And everybody knows you don't get a hole in one without help from above. God's just playing tricks and you merely went along for the ride. Besides, I can't take any more of this, so now get back to the woman's tee where you belong."

We all chuckled and played on.

Tom Biber, the owner of the course, was in the clubhouse at the time and saw all the commotion on the green. When we finished the game and went inside, he asked what had happened. We told him the story.

Lowell continued his hassling. "Who ever gets a hole in one is supposed to buy a round of drinks," he said.

The girls all came to my defense and insisted that Lowell buy the drinks. And in his customary generous manner he agreed, and treated us to a round of lemonade. And the celebration began!

*Divine Master, we thank You for the peak
       experiences in our lives.
       It is in moments like these that we
       feel a profound
       sense of Your personal love.
       These highs sustain us and
       encourage us to continue.
       Thank You
       for thrilling experiences.*

Three months later, Jackie had the ball
mounted on a beautiful plaque which read:

ON THE 28TH DAY OF JUNE 1994

DOROTHY K. EDERER

APPROACHED THE 10TH HOLE AT

RIDGEVIEW GOLF COURSE.

SHE TOOK A 5 WOOD OUT OF HER

BAG AND SMACKED THIS VERY BALL 155 YARDS.

AT 2:23 P.M. IT WAS DECLARED:

A HOLE IN ONE.

SOME SAY IT WAS "DIVINE INTERVENTION."

Prayers and Reflections for the Golfer

Opening Prayer

Wise Master, we enter Your presence to ask
   Your forgiveness
   for the times we failed to stay on course.
We have come upon rough times,
    we have fallen into sandy traps
    and strayed into
    barren wasteland and murky waters,
    all because of our handicap.
    Forgive us, God.

Help us to avoid the traps of feeling that we
    must always play a perfect game,
    always on par,
    or of being depressed when our game
    is below expectations.

We are often tempted to give up,
    when we go off course
    and in the rough,
    failing to trust You'll guide us
    back into play.
As we continue on the way,
    we still hook and slice,
        rather than follow the straight way.

We are fearful of what lies ahead,
    especially when we approach a dogleg.
In time we will learn to trust You.

Help us to be aware of the divots we make
    in life,
        and how often we fail to replace them,
        hoping no one will notice.

As we continually start anew,
    give us the grace to plant our feet
    firmly on the ground,
    face the right direction,
    and steady with our heads down
    and still,
    swing slow.
May we concentrate on following through
    as we drive forward
    with renewed intent.

Give us strength to face ourselves honestly and
    not be discouraged by our handicap.

May we have the assurance that, although
    we did not make par,
    or hit a hole in one,
    You will still welcome us
    into the clubhouse,
    where all struggling golfers,
    even duffers,
    are welcome to
    Your party at the nineteenth hole.

Words of Encouragement

Because you are God's chosen one,
    holy and beloved,
    clothe yourselves with heartfelt
    mercy,
    with kindness, humility,
    meekness, and patience.
Bear with one another;
    forgive whatever grievances
    you have against one another.
Forgive as the Lord has forgiven you.
Over all these virtues put on love,
    which binds the rest together
    and makes them perfect.

The Master's peace must reign in your
    hearts,
    since as members of the one body
    you have been called to that peace.
Dedicate yourselves to thankfulness.

Let the Master's word,
*   rich as it is, dwell in you.*
In wisdom made perfect,
*   instruct*
*   and admonish*
*   one another.*

Sing gratefully to God from your hearts
*   in psalms, hymns,*
*   and inspired songs.*

Whatever you do, whether in speech
*   or in action,*
*   do it in the name of the Lord.*

—COLOSSIANS 3:12–17

Personal Reflections

HANDICAP

Based on our average score

Whatever our handicap, it should never be an excuse for doing less than our best. May we not be discouraged by our handicaps. They often provide the push we need to accomplish heroic undertakings, which will affect the lives of others significantly.

Divine Master, I pray that I can accept my
*   handicap*
*   and not let it distract me.*
Restore in me faith to believe in myself again.
Surround me with Your love and grace.
Continue to give me the courage and desire
*   to love and*
*   serve others the way You do.*

TEE
Things we set ourselves up for

RIDICULE OR PRAISE

We each long for praise in things we do well, regardless of the situation or circumstance. We cannot ignore the need for affirmation and encouragement.

Each time we are praised for something we've done well, most often we become better. We often become what people expect of us.

The same is true of ridicule. It can drag us down and undermine our confidence. Sometimes we may even question our value as a person. So often when we are mean and nasty, it is because we are hurting. Knowing we are loved and accepted for who we are makes a great difference.

Our game can be seriously affected if we've had an argument with someone we value, or are worried about something that's happening in our life.

BLAME OR SHAME

Shame is feeling bad about who we are. It develops out of our perception of what others think of us. So often when we are shamed, we blame others, because we are disappointed in ourselves. There is a sense of shame that happens to us when we blame others, mostly because we haven't been able to accept responsibility for our actions. But in time we will learn, grow, and become the person we want to be. We can overcome our shame if we recognize our mistakes and work to conquer them.

Divine Master, as I open my heart to Your love,
may I praise and affirm my partner
and see the goodness
which stems
from a right relationship with You.
Heal me of any painful memories, and help me
to avoid hurting others
when I've been betrayed.
May I anticipate with joy what You have
in store for me as
I journey down the fairway to healing.

DOGLEG

A Major turn in our path

SICKNESSES
LOSS OF A JOB
LOSS OF A LOVED ONE

Our sicknesses and losses weigh heavily on our minds and hearts, but we learn something from each of them. Some losses may seem unbearable. Usually people who have suffered most are the ones who are the most compassionate. When we lose a job or a loved one, it takes time and patience to adjust. The healing process begins gradually as we learn to let go.

We never know what lies ahead, but if we put our trust in God, it makes sickness and loss a little easier to accept.

Divine Master, I welcome Your presence into
        every situation
        I will face today.
May those who cross my path experience Your
        joy and love.
Encourage me to accept whatever losses may
        come my way.

HOOKS AND SLICES

Depending on our aim, we may be hitting some
good shots, but in the wrong direction. The
Master will allow us to start fresh at any point in
our life. It is never too late to get our life back on
course, no matter what may have thrown us off
course.

Divine Master, sometimes we feel
        we're aiming right,
        but after a few strokes
        our sights are misdirected.
Forgive me for the times I've strayed from You.
Increase my sensitivity to others as I walk
        through life.

SAND TRAP

Things in life difficult to overcome

PERFECTIONISM

> *The game of golf is a game of accepting failure; of accepting imperfection; of realizing that the perfect game has never been played, never will be played, or ever could be played.*
>
> —Author Unknown

God doesn't expect us to be perfect, only to strive for it. God is patient with our mistakes. God may not like some of the things we do, but God is never disappointed in who we are, as long as we are trying and doing our best. If we are expecting ourselves to be perfect, we will only become anxious. In striving for perfection, it is important that we love ourselves as we are, and accept our strengths and weaknesses as we become aware of them. Becoming aware of our weaknesses can be uncomfortable at first, but it is the first step in

taking giant strides to becoming more loving
and forgiving.

UNREALISTIC EXPECTATIONS

We often expect more of ourselves than we do
of others. It's good to set goals, but make them
realistic and attainable. We have to be careful
not to expect more from ourselves than we are
capable of. It can dampen our spirit. God loves
us the way we are. We can still love ourselves
as we are and work hard for change.

DECEIT

When someone is not honest, it usually springs
from the fear of being rejected. We may hold
back the truth or something important, thinking
it will not harm the relationship, but it does not
always help us or others. Deceit has often
destroyed marriages, lost jobs, and soured relationships. Bertha Conde expressed it so well
when she said, "Every friendship that lasts is built
of certain durable materials. The first of these is
truthfulness. If I can look into the eyes of my
friend and always speak out the truthful thought

and feeling with the simplicity of a little child, there will be a real friendship between us." I am convinced that a relationship built on truthfulness has more chances of surviving than one which is not. We all desire to be loved and accepted. It is much easier to accept and forgive a person who is humble enough to speak the truth to us, even when it hurts. We will be respected more because of our honesty. We may fail to realize we are deceiving others by not counting all our strokes, but we are only hurting ourselves.

HYPOCRISY

Do we blame others for something we ourselves do? Example: An individual is upset because his partner failed to count a stroke when he retrieved his ball from the woods, and placed it on the fairway. That same person turns around and moves his ball away from a tree, because it was impossible to hit, but refused to count it as a stroke. Most of the time, we become angry or upset when we see traits in others we ourselves possess.

*   *   *

What *sand traps* have slowed you down
spiritually? Reflect on these words of
Max Lucado:

> Faith has its share of bunkers,
> and golf has its share of prayers.

Divine Master, often I feel I have to do
> *everything perfectly to*
> *receive Your love, but I know You will*
> *always love me, even*
> *when I don't always do my best.*
> *I will continue to forgive*
> *and love myself*
> *as I work toward changing*
> *those things that make me*
> *the person*
> *You would like me to be.*
> *I will strive always to be*
> *honest with myself*
> *and others*
> *as I speak the truth,*
> *even if no one listens,*

even if no one understands why.
As I become aware of my weaknesses,
may I also be more
aware of Your eternal love for me.

OUT OF BOUNDS

Success in life or in golf depends upon how concentrated our focus is. Sometimes we act quickly, fail to concentrate, and end up off course or in rough places.

Divine Master, I recognize the times I have
        stayed from You.
Forgive me for the pain I have caused others
        because of my weaknesses.
May I return, through your grace and love, to
        live my life on the
        path of goodness.
Thank You for your mercy.
        Help me focus
        and concentrate
        on what I am doing in life.

WATER HOLES
Situations difficult to get out of

PAINFUL RELATIONSHIPS

We may find ourselves denying that the relationship we are in is not healthy for either of us. We do it as a way of protecting ourselves. We refuse to acknowledge the reality until we feel prepared to cope with the situation. Some of us need time to prepare ourselves and figure out how we will cope. People can scream the truth, but unless we are ready to listen, we may not make a wise choice.

In golf, it is extremely difficult to concentrate on the game if someone is constantly giving suggestions or correcting a play. It's not so much what one may be saying, but how it is said. Some people fight more on a golf course than anywhere else.

DEPRESSION

We may be depressed for a number of reasons:
1. When we fail to obtain that which we seek.
2. When we can't live up to our expectations.

3. When another has what we want.

4. When we compare ourself to others.

We want to do our best. A bad shot or a high score can spoil our day. We need to learn not to take the game so seriously. Golf is a sport to be enjoyed. We do better when we are relaxed.

REJECTION BY OTHERS

If we expect everyone to love us, we will never be happy. No matter how good we are, or how famous we are, all of us at some time in our lives have experienced rejection. Even the Master was rejected. We can't expect better for ourselves.

INJUSTICES (EITHER TO YOU OR SOMEONE YOU LOVE)

Whenever we find ourselves angry or irritated with someone, it may not be the person but something about ourselves that bothers us. So often we hurt others because we are hurting.

We don't like to see injustice in a sport. Being human, we'll make mistakes, stumble and fall

along the fairway of life, but it's how we pick
ourselves up and go on that is important to
the Master.

How have you responded to the water holes
in your life? Reflect on these words of
Lee Trevino:

> There are two things you can do
> with your head down, play golf
> and pray.

Divine Master, sometimes I fail to respond
> *lovingly to the*
> *water holes in my life.*
> *Help me to listen*
> *as I make wise choices*
> *on how to live my life*
> *more for You.*
Relationships can be painful, but when You are
> *the center of them, those painful and*
> *stressful times*
> *become easier.*

Teach me how to deal with depression
and not allow it
to consume my spirit.
Heal my wounds and strengthen me
as I continue to
pick myself up and keep trying.
When I experience rejection, may it cause me to
reflect on my life
and realize that I
am a good person
and I am loved.

Driver or Putter?

We live in a world where success sometimes is viewed more important than family or friends. We may spend more time getting ahead and less time developing friendships and bonding with our family. Or we can trust the Master, who has a hand in it all, and accept what comes our way as part of the game.

Divine Master, may I never let success or fame
be my goal,
but strive always to be in a right
relationship with You
as I putt along through life.

A Mulligan

God always gives us second chances. We are given the right to be human, to be weak, to stumble and fall, but as long as we continue to reach out and forgive not only those who hurt us, but also ourselves, we are pleasing in the Master's eyes. When we find it in our heart to forgive and realize that what someone did to us was a result of weakness, imperfection, and impatience, then we free ourselves. As long as we harbor anger and resentment, we will never be free. Our prayer life will lack power, our jobs and relationships will be affected, and our health will suffer. We all want a second chance; let's pray we will give it to others.

Divine Master, often You have given me
　　　second chances.
Forgive me for the times I've refused
　　　to give others the same.
Help me to be sensitive to others
　　　who are hurting.
Increase my vision to see the pain and
　　　brokenness in others.
Keep me meek in offering my opinion.
Teach me how to forgive myself when I offend
　　　someone.
Transform me into the person I am to become.

Closing Prayer

Wise Master, in the Game of Life
You know that though most of us are duffers,
    we all aspire to be champions.
Help us, we pray, to be grateful for the course,
    including both the fairways and the rough.

Thank You for those who have made it possible
    for us to tee off.
Thank You for the thrill of a solid, soaring drive,
    the challenge of the dogleg,
    the trial of the trap,
    the discipline of the water hazard,
    and the beauty of a cloudless sky.

Thank You, God, our Master and Pro,
    who shows us how to get the right grip
    on life,
    to slow down our back swing,
    to correct our crazy hooks and slices,
    to keep our heads down in humility,
    and to follow through in self-control.

Teach us also to be good sports
> who will accept the rub of the green,
> the penalty for wandering out of
> bounds,
> the reality of lost balls,
> the relevancy of par,
> and the dangers of the nineteenth hole.

And when our last putt
> has dropped into the cup,
> and the light of our last day
> has faded into darkness,
> though our trophies be few,
> our handicap still too high,
> and, for most of us,
> the hole in one still only a dream,
> may we be able to turn in to You,
> our tournament director at the great
> clubhouse,
> an honest scorecard.
> > Amen.

—AUTHOR UNKNOWN.

ADAPTED BY DOROTHY K. EDERER

Beatitudes
for the Golfer

Happy the golfer whose drive is firm and aim
     is straight;
     she will find herself better positioned
     to reach her goal.

Happy the golfer who repairs his divot;
     those who follow will bless him.

Happy the golfer who is constantly counseled
     by the worst player on the team,
     for she will make giant drives in
     patience.

Happy the golfer whose drive strikes
     the cart path;
     she will find herself far ahead of the others.

Happy the golfer who patiently waits his turn
     on the green,
     for he shall be blessed by all.

Happy the golfer who is not envious when
     his partner's tee is halfway
     up the fairway;
     he can rejoice when others do well.

Happy the honest scorekeeper;
     though he may lose the game,
     he is still a winner.

Happy the woman who in a single shot
     drives the ball home
     from the lofty men's tee;
     she will be called awesome.

Happy the one whose ball grazes
     the head of a swimming muskrat
     and lands upon the fairway.
     Truly blessed is that person,
     though no one believes the story
     as it is continually retold.

Happy the golfer to whom strange things have
     happened;
          it manifests the playfulness of God.

Happy the golfer who walks the links with his
     family;
          their life together will be truly blessed.

Psalms for the
Golfer

Psalm 1
True Happiness

Happy the one who follows not the counsel
     of beginners,
     nor looks down upon the lowly,
     nor speaks while others take careful aim,
     but delights when someone pars,
     or even better, makes a birdie.

And is not envious
     when someone aces
     or plays a perfect game.

Such a person is like an eagle in the air,
     that soars above the less thoughtful
     and thrives in difficult situations,
     he is consistent on whatever course he
     plays.
Even when he loses, he wins.

Psalm 16:7-11 Prayer Against Opponents

I bless my God, my Guide, who counsels me,
    even in a hazard my heart exalts You.

I place the ball before me, with You at my right,
    I shall not go astray.
My heart is glad, my spirit rejoices,
    my body too relaxes in confidence.

Because You will not allow the ball to go into
    strange or desolate places,
    nor will You allow a brand-new ball to
    sink in muddy waters.

You show me the sure way home
    along a crooked fairway,
    and fullness of joy when I arrive.
You delight when on a rare occasion
    my ball strikes the pin and falls
    gently into the hole.

Psalm 18:2-4, 7
Thanksgiving for
Help and Victory

I love You, my Guide,
        You are my strength and comfort.

You give me confidence as I
        choose the appropriate instrument
        for the fairway stroke.

I praise You, God, for You protect me
        from the hazards in life.

In my distress I so often called upon You.
      How often You came to assist me
         when I drifted into four-foot-high bunkers.

From a distance You knew my need
      and immediately came to my aid.
You are always by my side to guide and uphold me.

I love You, O God, my Counsel and Guide.

Psalm 23 The Lord Is My Guide

The Lord is my guide, I shall not worry.
   In verdant courses He sets my feet.
From dangerous waters He leads me,
   refreshing my spirit.

He guides me on straight paths
   for a clearer aim.
Even though at times I end up in rough places,
   I have no fears, for the gentle Master
   is there to help me.

With my woods and irons
   I progress from tee to greens
   with hope and exultation.

You created the beautiful landscape before me
        to be enjoyed with all my friends.

You bless my putter with good fortune, and I
        will accomplish the unthinkable.
Only blessings and happiness follow me,
        though awards and trophies may not
        always await me.

But I shall forever rejoice on
        the nineteenth green,
        where my family will celebrate with me.

Psalm 37 The Fate of Cheaters and the Reward of the Honest

Do not grow angry with those who are
        dishonest
        in their count,
        or envy those who knock it stiff.
For as quick as you can spray a shot,
        you can also make an eagle.

Put your trust in God and you will improve.
Resting secure on your course, you will fare well.
Take delight in your Guide,
        and reserve a place for God
        in your heart,
        for God ultimately grants you
        your heart's desire.

Commit all your strokes to the Divine
   and be confident.
The gentle Master will be ever present to you.

Stay silent around others and wait patiently
   your turn.
Do not become riled when a poor player
   unjustly counts strokes,
   and plays unfairly,
   for he knows in his heart
   it is the only way he can win against you.

Be not angry or upset,
   you will lose your concentration.
But stay calm and focused,
   and you will ultimately surpass him
   and win the game.

Psalm 54 Confident Prayer in God

Divine Master, help me in the "Skins game"
       and with Your power
       and strength direct me.

Hear my plea for confidence as I
       address the ball
       with my ginty.

Arrogant golfers may make fun of me;
       jokesters may try to distract me,
       thinking to throw me off my game.

But You will guide me and keep me focused,
       for You delight when I make it
       on the green
       and reassure me as I try my best.

After each hole I will praise You,
       for Your goodness and love
       are my companions.

You have rescued me from many hazards
       along the way.
As I trust in You for help,
       may others look to me for help
       along the way.

Psalm 62 Trust in God Alone

In my Guide alone does my spirit trust.
Each step along the fairway, my God is there.

God is like a shade
      against the scorching noonday sun
      and like a cool breeze on a sultry day.
God's presence is sure as a rock on soft ground.

I ask God's pardon for those who never
      play fair;
      I know God watches their every stroke.

How long will my friendly foursome last
      when rules of courtesy are not observed,
      or when one drives for show
      and putts only
      for dough?

I rest in my Guide, who will see me through.

When the game is over, still will I laugh,
        for the game was fun
            though I may not have won.

God is my shield and safety when I come
            close to the woods.
God is my strength when my drive
            went far along the fairway, well over
            two hundred yards.
I knew God was beside me giving me help.

The Golfer's Ten Commandments

1. The Divine Master will always be
number one,
thy family second, and golf third.

2. God's name will be used only to praise.

3. Every day will be holy, with the Master
as thy partner.

4. Thou shall not pick up golf balls while
they are still rolling.

5. Thou shall not try to kill the ball;
an easy stroke will take it farther.

6. Thou shall not steal tees or balls from your partner's golf bag.

7. Thou shall count all thy strokes.

8. Thou shall witness thy partner's birdie, which landed one inch from the hole.

9. Thou shall not covet thy partner's score.

10. Thou shall not covet thy neighbor's golf sweaters.

The Prayer of
Saint Francis
for the Golfer

$\mathcal{L}$ord, make us honest golfers on the course.
Where jealousy appears,
       help us affirm one another's gifts.
Where unkind words are spoken,
       teach us to forgive.
Where others doubt their ability,
       help us praise and support.
Where there is despair,
       may we give them encouragement.
Where there is darkness,
       let us be the spark to brighten their day.
And where there is sadness,
       inspire us to be joyful.

Divine Master, grant that we may not seek
        so much to be the best player
        as to be grateful to You
        for the gifts and talents we possess;
To be calm when others are upset;
To be respectful to those we walk
        the course with.

For it is in giving our best that we receive life.
It is in overlooking faults and weaknesses
        of others
        that You will be compassionate
        toward us.

It is in dying to our ego that we may become
        the person You intended us to be.

Praise for
A Golfer's Day with the Master:

"Dorothy Ederer and her new book, *A Golfer's Day with the Master*, truly capture the spirit of golf, but more importantly, the spirit of the Master in His desire for us to play and live in His Grip. It will bring the golfer closer to par, as well as closer to the Master through its wonderful golf stories, prayers and reflections. It is a book that will strengthen your faith as you walk down the fairway of life. It's a perfect gift for all those who love the game."

—Wally Armstrong, PGA Tour, Coauthor, In His Grip, Playing the Game

"After reading *A Golfer's Day with the Master* I realized how very fortunate I have been to be able to have spent my career working in the golf industry. Sr. Dorothy's enthusiasm for the game of golf, and her commitment to faith, is very contagious."

—Andrew C. Mears, PGA Member, Vice President of Golf Card International

"Sr. Dorothy's words are like a round on Augusta . . . peaceful, beautiful, challenging and memorable."

—*Monsignor Tom Hartman,*
Director of Communication for the Diocese
of Rockville Center, Long Island,
Television Show "God Squad"

"It's a wonderful book. I read it in one sitting. A positive look at life's challenges. A new rule book for the Game of Life."

—*Mike Olizarevitch, C.P.G.A.,*
Golf Professional and Manager of Fanchawe
Golf Course
London, Ontario, Canada